Everything You Need to Know to

Raise Money

(and Have Fun) with a Charity Auction

An Insider's Guide to the Ins, Outs,
Ups and Downs of a Profitable Event

The Gold Standard in Books for Nonprofit Boards

Read each in an hour • Quantity discounts up to 45 percent

Fund Raising Realities Every Board Member Must Face
David Lansdowne, 112 pp., $24.95, ISBN 1889102326

Nearly 100,000 board members and development officers have used this book to help them raise substantial money – in sluggish and robust economies. Have your board spend just *one* hour with this classic and they'll come to understand virtually everything they need to know about raising big gifts.

Asking Jerold Panas, 112 pp., $24.95, ISBN 1889102350

It ranks right up there with public speaking. Nearly all of us fear it. And yet it's critical to our success. *Asking for money*. This landmark book convincingly shows that nearly everyone, regardless of their persuasive ability, can become an effective fundraiser if they follow Jerold Panas' step-by-step guidelines.

The Ultimate Board Member's Book
Kay Sprinkel Grace, 120 pp., $24.95, ISBN 1889102393

A book for *all* nonprofit boards: those wanting to operate with maximum effectiveness, those needing to clarify exactly what their job is, and, those wanting to ensure that all members are 'on the same page.' It's all here in jargon-free language: how boards work, what the job entails, the time commitment, the role of staff, effective recruiting, de-enlisting board members, and more.

The 11 Questions Every Donor Asks
Harvey McKinnon, 112 pp., $24.95, ISBN 1889102377

A watershed book, *The 11 Questions* prepares you for the tough questions you'll inevitably face from prospective donors. Harvey McKinnon identifies 11 such questions, ranging from "Why me?" to "Will my gift make a difference?" to "Will I have a say over how you use my gift?" And the suggested answers are illuminating.

How Are We Doing? Gayle Gifford, 120 pp., $24.95, ISBN 1889102237

Until now, almost all books dealing with board evaluation have had an air of unreality about them. The perplexing graphs, the matrix boxes, the overlong questionnaires. Enter Gayle Gifford, who has pioneered an elegantly simple way for your board to evaluate and improve its overall performance. It all comes down to answering a host of simple, straightforward questions.

Big Gifts for Small Groups
Andy Robinson, 112 pp., $24.95, ISBN 1889102210

If yours is among the thousands of organizations for whom six- and seven-figure gifts are unattainable, then in this book you'll learn everything you need to know to secure big gifts: how to get ready for the campaign; whom to approach; how to ask; what to do once you have the commitment; even how to convey your thanks in a memorable way.

Emerson & Church, Publishers
www.emersonandchurch.com

Everything You Need to Know to

Raise Money

(and Have Fun) with a Charity Auction

An Insider's Guide to the Ins, Outs,
Ups and Downs of a Profitable Event

ROBERT BAIRD

Emerson
& Church
PUBLISHERS

First printed in September 2009

Printed in the United States of America

ISBN 1-889102-36-9

10 9 8 7 6 5 4 3 2 1

This text is printed on acid-free paper.

Copies of this book are available from the
publisher at discount when purchased in
quantity for boards of directors or staff.

Emerson & Church, Publishers
28A Park Street • Medfield, MA 02052
Tel. 508-359-0019 • www.emersonandchurch.com

Library of Congress Cataloging-in-Publication Data

Baird, Robert, 1957-
 Everything you need to know to raise money (and have fun)
with a charity auction : an insider's guide to the ins, outs, ups
and downs of a profitable event / by Robert Baird.
  p. cm.
 ISBN 978-1-889102-36-8 (pbk. : alk. paper)
 1. Benefit auctions. I. Title.
 HF5476.B25 2009
 658.15'224—dc22

                                   2009022395

To my wife, Laura,
and my daughters Emily and Allison

Also by Emerson & Church

Going for the Green!
An Insider's Guide to Raising Money with Charity Golf, by Tom King

How profitable is golf as a fundraiser? The numbers speak for themselves.

According to the National Golf Foundation:

• An estimated 140,000 charity tournaments take place each year ...

• Drawing 15 million players ...

• And raising a gulp-inducing sum of $3 billion for everything from cancer research to special education.

In other words, if your organization isn't hosting a golf tournament, chances are another agency down the block is – and realizing anywhere from $10,000 to $250,000 in sponsorships and player registrations.

If you're late to the tee and want to launch your own tournament, or enhance an existing one, then Tom King's new book, *Going for the Green!*, is a 300-yard drive straight down the middle.

King covers everything an organizer needs to know: when to start your planning; how to attract players; recruiting the right volunteers; the costs involved; choosing the best format; adding spice to your event; when to schedule it; how to secure sponsors; how to computerize the process; how to cope with the myriad details on tournament day; and how to evaluate your event to make it better next year.

Another notable strength of *Going for the Green!* is its extensive appendix. King is so committed to making your event a success that he offers a slew of tip sheets including: a checklist of tasks you need to accomplish from six months out; a budget worksheet; a description of different tournament formats; seventeen job descriptions for specific volunteers; a look at some quirky formats; sample sponsorship levels; a description of sidebar events to add interest; and even a glossary for neophytes.

Going for the Green!
156 pp., ISBN 9781889102382, $24.95.

www.emersonandchurch.com

CONTENTS

1   Is a Charity Auction Right for You?   9

2   Getting Started   13

3   Committees   21

4   Setting Your Budget   29

5   Publicity   33

6   The Timeline   37

7   How It All Works   41

8   The Auction Catalog   47

9   The Auction Program   51

10 Checking In   55

11 The Silent Auction   57

12 The Live Auction   61

13 Additional Revenue Sources   73

14 The Big Night   77

15 Auction Software and Online Auctions   81

    A Last Word   85

    Appendix   87-141

1

Is a Charity Auction Right for You?

It was Francis Bacon who said, "A prudent question is one-half of wisdom."

With that in mind, let's start with the most basic of queries: Why hold a fundraising auction?

Well, maybe a board member suggested it at the last meeting. Or perhaps a group on the other side of town raises gazillions with their auction, or so you hear. Or maybe you're just plain tired of Hopscotch for Health (or whatever your long-standing annual event is called).

I don't have to tell you that these are all weak reasons to forge ahead.

In my experience, most, or at least far too many, organizations plan an auction without asking themselves three essential questions:

"Do we have enough time to prepare?" The absolute minimum is nine months; a year is better.

"Can we recruit sufficient volunteers?" You'll need dozens, even for a small auction.

"Does an auction make sense for us?" That depends on your answers to the preceding questions, the

Rolodexes of your board, and the health of the economy in your area.

Some public elementary schools raise more than $10,000 with auctions (about 200 attendees and 200 to 300 items). Private schools use auctions, raising $50,000 to $150,000 per year. And organizations of all stripes – from museums to hospitals to YMCAs – have enjoyed different levels of success.

Of course, that doesn't mean your auction will do as well, especially if it's your first attempt. But with a can-do attitude, some common sense, a few hearty laughs, and taking to heart the tips offered in this book, your event, just like the bids, will soar beyond your expectations.

■ How a fundraising auction works (in a nutshell)

If you've attended an auction, you know it can be a great social event – sometimes dinner is even included. Usually the auction has a theme and most last three to four hours. Generally, there are two components: a silent auction and a live auction.

The silent auction is held first and serves as a "warm up." It's where you sell donated goods that aren't expected to fetch large sums of money. The live auction is the main event where high-value gifts are auctioned to the highest bidder.

Approximately one year before the big night, an auction committee is formed and a chair is named. If you're lucky enough to be this individual, hang on to your hat – your mettle will soon be tested.

Working with the leadership of your organization,

you'll pick a date, place, and theme. You'll name members to chair the major committees such as acquisition, decoration, and finance and in turn they'll recruit volunteers to fill their committees.

The number of volunteers you'll need depends on the size of your auction. But don't be fooled: even a small auction can require a small army of 20 to 30 volunteers. Not everyone will have major roles or formally serve on a committee, but your volunteer base should have tentacles so that it's able to accomplish tasks small and large. If you don't feel you and your committee can recruit these kinds of numbers, better to beg off now and opt for a different event.

Volunteers serving on the Acquisition Committee canvass the area in search of gifts from local businesses and residents. The gifts are catalogued, stored, valued, and ultimately transported to the event. Meanwhile, other volunteers are preparing invitations, flyers, welcome packets, and devising plans for decorating the auction venue.

Once the big night arrives, guests will check in and receive a registration packet containing the auction catalog, door-prize tickets, and other miscellaneous items. They'll enter and find a beautifully decorated room overflowing with gifts on which they can bid during the silent auction. They'll spend much of their time socializing and tracking the progress of their bids.

Once the silent auction is closed, the guests will be seated and the real fun will begin. The live auction will last one to two hours and a professional auctioneer or a volunteer from your organization will auction off

11

approximately 25 to 75 items. If you've done your work, most of them will be irresistible to the bidders.

After the live auction is finished, your guests will proceed to the checkout tables, unless you've implemented an automatic payment system. They'll pay for and pick up their items, and leave with a smile on their face, assuming your committee has done a good job.

■ What should your goal be?

That all depends, of course, on factors such as your experience, the size of your organization, the affluence of your membership, the state of the economy, not to mention how well you've planned the event. Any and all of these will determine your potential profits.

If you've held auctions before, you already have a sense of how much you can raise. Perhaps your goal will be an amount slightly larger than last year's. But beware of limiting yourself this way, especially if you have a good volunteer crew. Maybe you've been under-achieving without realizing it!

If this is your very first auction, I'd follow the advice of Olympian Peggy Fleming: "The ultimate goal should be doing your best and enjoying it."

In other words, forget about setting a dollar goal.

If you haven't tried the techniques discussed in this book, you can't really estimate how well you'll do. So don't even try. Simply have fun and get the experience of running an auction under your belt. Then, the next time out, you'll have a pretty good idea of your potential to raise $10,000 or $100,000.

2

Getting Started

It was Harry Truman who said, "Whenever I make a bum decision, I go out and make another one."

With due respect to our 33rd President, I'm hoping the big decisions you and your key players make, and make early, will be sound ones. Each of them will set the tone for your event and ultimately your success.

■ Choosing a location

Deciding where to hold your auction is the first order of business. There are several factors to keep in mind, paramount among them are cost and size. If your organization owns or has access to a site large enough to hold your auction, the decision is easy. If not, you'll have to look into renting a room or rooms for the event.

Many of your options are obvious: Knights of Columbus hall, Moose Lodge, VFW hall, local school auditorium, gymnasium, firehouse, and hotel ballroom. Then, too, I was once involved with an auction held on the lanai at the Hickham Air Force Base Officers Club overlooking beautiful Pearl Harbor. Talk about a location!

The site you choose must be large enough to accommodate both your silent and live auction. You may want to consider using two rooms (if your location has an elevated stage or podium, one room might suffice). Your silent auction should be set up to allow for maximum "milling around." Remember, the silent auction is a social event. For the live auction, however, you'll need to have seats for your guests. A quick room change is possible, but you'll need an intermission to accomplish this.

If you're renting a location, be sure to reserve it early, secure a contract that discusses details such as time of access, set-up responsibility, cleanup, number of tables, chairs, sound system, podium or lecterns, portable stage, decoration restrictions, and catering. In Appendix P I've included a checklist of things to consider when renting a hall.

> **TIP**: As the big day draws near, perhaps at the intervals of six months, three months, and one month, confirm with your site that everything is on track. Nothing is worse than finding out a month before your event that there was a misunderstanding about your reservation or room assignment.

■ Choosing a date

Choosing a date is as important as choosing a location. Often, these two decisions are tied together for obvious reasons. Most auctions are held either in the spring or fall. Summer is generally a bad time since many of your prospective guests will be vacationing. Winter isn't advantageous either, as many are preparing for or recovering from the holidays.

Of the two seasons, fall is generally your best bet. Many of your guests will be getting into the holiday shopping mood and may find that what you have to offer is on their shopping list. I myself have purchased (and placed under the Christmas tree) vacation and ski packages for my family. Weekend evenings are the most popular time since most auctions last well into the night.

■ Picking a theme

Using a theme can add to the fun of your auction. It allows you to create a "buzz" around what would normally be seen as just another fundraising event. It also puts people in a good mood and can loosen their grip on their wallets. A theme also provides direction for your Decoration Committee. Some of the themes I've seen used are Margaritaville, Hurray to Hollywood, Havana Nights, and Hee Haw. Some other popular general themes include a Masquerade, a Rock and Roll Party, a Disco Party, Winter Wonderland, Mardi Gras, and a Medieval Night.

Searching the Internet is an easy way to generate ideas for a theme. Here are some good links:

www.alltimefavorites.com/nationwide/theme_ideas/
www.partydirectory.com/guide/ptytheme.htm
www.themepartiesnmore.com
www.spritzels.com/party/list.html

■ Choosing an auctioneer

You'll need to decide whether to hire a professional auctioneer or use a volunteer (if you're really lucky, you might have a volunteer who IS a professional auctioneer).

Professionals will cost you more, at least up front, but they'll move more gifts and for more money. A professional can auction approximately 35 items in an evening, at 20 to 25 percent higher prices than an amateur can. A professional can also provide consulting services, training, paddles, software, and forms. However, you'll pay between $1,500 to $2,500 for these services.

If yours is a small auction, it might be wise to use a volunteer. The same is true if you have a volunteer with a magnetic personality and is known by many of your guests. This can give your event a casual and personal feel. Although an amateur may only move 15 to 20 items in an evening, he or she will be able to interject local humor a professional can't. Be aware, however, that with a volunteer auctioneer the evening can (and often does) run late. So make sure expectations and timing are clear.

I once had a volunteer auctioneer come out in a cow costume, udders and all. It was totally unexpected but it worked. However, as the co-chair, I wasn't aware it was going to happen and it could have turned sour (no pun intended).

You always want to know what the auctioneer is planning.

Another example: Not long ago, I attended an auction where a professional auctioneer asked each guest to plunk $20 on the table. He then played a game where at the end only one person was left standing. This individual won half of the total take. It sounds like fun, right, and a little extra money for the organization? The problem was that neither the organizers nor the guests knew they would be asked to spend $20 above and beyond the $100 ticket price they'd already paid. And more than a few were peeved.

> **TIP**: You can learn more about professional auctioneers, including how to locate one in your area, by visiting the website of the National Auctioneers Association (www.auctioneers.org). The site also contains links to companies providing auction supplies. Lastly, many states have auction associations. Google "auction association" + your state.

■ Casual, formal, or something in-between

Whether your event is black-tie or denim is entirely up to you. There are pros and cons to either choice. Your key consideration should be the people you want to attract. If your audience is your own membership, then you already have a feel for what would be appropriate.

On the other hand, if you're attempting to attract an audience from the community at large, you and your committee will need to assess what the market will bear. So much depends on where you're located, your competition, the cause, and your ability to attract guests based on your committee's personal contacts.

You do need to have this discussion early, as it will

affect the theme you choose, your advertising, the design of your invitations, whether your event is catered, whether you have an open or "no host" bar, and the price of admission.

■ Refreshments

You generally have four options when it comes to food and drink: dinner, hors d'oeuvres, dessert, and beverages. What you offer will be a function of what your guests typically expect and what admission price you think they're willing to pay. Your other decision about refreshments will be whether to have any or all of them catered.

If you use a professional caterer, make sure you understand the contract. Ask about any hidden costs and at what point the number of guests needs to be finalized. Also, ask what contingencies are available if the guest list grows unexpectedly. If your caterers are providing bar services, make sure you have a clear understanding of all costs, including corkage and bartender fees, and whether the caterer is using licensed professionals.

One last note: unless you have refreshments catered (and built into the cost of admission), try to get them donated. Local grocery markets, party supply stores, and caterers may be willing to donate refreshments and various supplies (napkins, cups) in exchange for being listed in your program.

■ Photography

If you want pictures or video taken at your auction,

you can either hire a professional photographer or enlist a volunteer. If neither of these options is available, make sure you have someone (even if it's your teenage son or daughter) taking pictures throughout the evening. These pictures will aid next year's committee members with planning and set-up.

■ Speeches

Heed Franklin Roosevelt's words when it comes to speeches at your auction: "Be sincere, be brief; be seated."

Remember, your guests didn't come to hear someone talk, they came to have fun and socialize. Give your speaker no more than 10 minutes, five is better. And choose *one* speaker, usually your Master of Ceremonies, Auction Chair, or organization President.

Items covered in a welcome speech should include: the reason you're holding the auction, a mention of major donors and sponsors, a thank-you to all volunteers (mentioning the names of committee chairs), and a plea to "give till it feels good." Remember, the purpose of the auction is to make money.

3

Committees

You've heard the jibes as I have:

"A committee is a body that keeps minutes and wastes hours."

"Meetings are indispensable when you don't want to do anything."

"To get something done a committee should consist of no more than three people, two of whom are absent."

Despite the disparagements, committees are essential, especially to an event as labor intensive as a charity auction.

The size of your auction will dictate the number and type of committees you need. Here, let's concentrate on the different committees you might form to make your event a rousing success.

■ The Auction Steering Committee

This committee consists of the Auction Chair and leaders of the other committees, or at least the major committees. The Auction Steering Committee will recommend the date, location, theme, choice of auctioneer, operating budget, and the price of admission.

For a large auction, the committee should hold its "kickoff" meeting no later than one year before the event. After that, the committee should meet monthly until three to four months before the auction. At that point, they'll likely need to meet every two weeks. Certainly, in the last month, the committee will be meeting weekly.

■ The Acquisition (Procurement) Committee

The Acquisition Committee is a required committee. Its purpose is to acquire, catalog, store, and track all gifts. During the early stages, this committee requires plenty of volunteers. Once you've logged a sufficient number of gifts and donations, some of the volunteers can shift their focus to other committees.

I recommend the committee meet frequently (possibly weekly or every two weeks) in the beginning so that members can share tips and provide encouragement.

The specifics of the acquisition process are discussed in detail in Chapter 5 - "How it all Works (The Processes)".

■ The Advertising Committee

The Advertising Committee is a required committee. Its purpose is to publicize the auction. This committee may also have responsibility for placing paid advertising and putting together the auction catalog or program (all discussed later).

The Advertising Committee needn't meet as frequently as other committees (monthly will do), unless it has the responsibility for cataloging items and developing the program. Your goal should be to recruit individuals with an advertising or marketing background, those with personal or professional contacts with local media, and those with graphic arts capabilities.

■ The Invitations/Reservations/Check in Committee

The Invitations/Reservations/Check in Committee, aside from being a committee with a very long name, is a required committee. The reason for the long title is that these three functions are usually performed by the same people but at different stages. The purpose of the committee is to send out the invitations (if used), collect and track the RSVP's and payment, and check-in guests on the night of the event.

This committee will need to meet frequently to draft and mail out the invitations. Once that's accomplished, they can convene every few weeks to compile the status of the RSVPs.

■ The Auction Catalog Committee

The Auction Catalog Committee is a required committee. Its purpose is to put together the auction catalog and possibly the auction program. However, the program itself could be a responsibility of the Advertising Committee. Again, this really depends on the size of your auction. The Auction Catalog Committee works closely with the Acquisition Committee to ensure that all donations are indexed and catalogued.

The Auction Catalog Committee will need to meet regularly, but not frequently until late in the auction cycle. At that point, the committee will be faced with late gift arrivals and catalog addendums.

■ The Silent Auction Committee

The Silent Auction Committee is a required committee. Its purpose is to ensure that all aspects of the silent auction run smoothly. This includes such things as deciding which items will be placed in the silent auction, setting the opening and minimum bids, determining how each item will be displayed, and overseeing the silent auction on auction night.

The Silent Auction Committee begins to meet as gifts are acquired by the Acquisition Committee. The frequency of their meetings will increase in the last few months.

■ The Live Auction Committee

The Live Auction Committee is a required committee. Its purpose is to ensure that all aspects of the live auction run smoothly. This includes: deciding which items will be placed in the live auction, recommending the opening bid amount, providing necessary information to the auctioneer, determining how items will be displayed, assisting with the live auction by serving as auction spotters and bid recorders, and participating in dispute resolution (should it be necessary).

Similar to the Silent Auction Committee, the Live Auction Committee begins meeting once gifts are acquired by the Acquisition Committee and the frequency of their meetings will increase in the last few months before the event.

■ The Publicity Committee

The Publicity Committee may not be a required committee. It depends on the size of your auction. If your auction is small, the Advertising Committee may perform the duties of the Publicity Committee. However, if your auction is large, you may want to devote a committee specifically to the promotion of the event, thereby freeing other members to focus on the logistics of the attendance list and checking in guests.

■ The Auction Checkout Committee

The Auction Checkout Committee is a required committee. As will be discussed later, the process of checking out guests (collecting payment, retrieving gifts, recording invoices) is a major task and can make a perfectly enjoyable evening a disaster if handled poorly. This committee needn't meet frequently, but should come together at least a couple of times early in the auction cycle, so they're aware of the exact processes that will be used. Closer to the big night, the committee will want to meet regularly to put all of the records in place and determine what roles volunteers will play in the checkout process.

■ The Decoration and Display Committee

The Decoration and Display Committee is a required committee. This group will meet early in the auction cycle to create a decoration plan consistent with the theme you've chosen. Once planning is in place, the committee won't need to meet until a few months before the auction to start acquiring the necessary materials (table skirts, centerpieces, backdrops, streamers, live auction paddle decorations, silent auction table dressing) and plan for the auction decoration activities.

■ The Miscellaneous Revenue Sources Committee

The Miscellaneous Revenue Sources Committee is not a required committee. Whether you choose to have one depends on the size of your auction. The responsibilities of this committee may include the coordination of raffles, door prizes, and possibly advertising (if not performed by the Advertising Committee).

■ The Thank You Committee

The Thank You Committee isn't a required committee but it is essential that someone do this work. Thank you letters need to be sent to those who contribute gifts very soon after the items are acquired (it's not a good idea to wait until after the auction is over).

Additionally, once the auction is complete, a thank you letter should go out to all contributors and attendees, announcing the auction's success and asking for their participation in future auctions. Further, other thank you letters will need to be drafted and mailed to auction volunteers, committee chairs, and other organizations that supported the event. This committee will start its activities shortly after the Acquisition Committee starts acquiring gifts.

■ The Finance Committee

The Finance Committee is not a required committee, but someone will need to keep a good accounting of all revenue and expenses (your current bookkeeper is a good candidate). Periodic meetings that describe the auction's status should always include a discussion of the financial statement (see Appendix T). At the very end of the auction, the financial statement serves as the measure of your auction's success.

•••

A few important things to think about. First, make sure that volunteers who are assigned to committees are suited to the work. For instance, it wouldn't make sense for an introvert to join the Acquisition Committee. However, he or she might excel on the Decorations or Finance Committee. Explain the functions of the different committees and allow volunteers to decide where they can best contribute.

Second, send out requests for volunteers, along with a description of the committee's responsibilities, early. It pays to know in advance who your interested volunteers are. They'll likely serve as your committee chairs and help you recruit other volunteers.

4

Setting Your Budget

"A budget," as one wag put it, "tells us what we can't afford, but it doesn't keep us from buying it."

But you've got more discipline than that, I'm sure. You're going to watch every last penny.

I often get asked, "How much will this cost?" and "How can we make sure we don't lose money?"

The only way to address these questions is to develop a budget, and that starts with projecting your expenses.

My advice, here and elsewhere, is to keep expenses to a minimum. That is, try to get everything donated. This might include rental for the location, paper products, bartending services, chairs and tables from the local church. You might even get a professional auctioneer, if he or she is a friend of your organization, to donate their services or at least offer a discount. There's very little that isn't a potential donation opportunity.

So what might you need to pay for?

- Location rental (hotel, hall, auditorium)
- Dinner (per plate)
- Bar (open or cash)

- Audio-visual equipment (sound, lighting, computers)
- Parking
- Auctioneer (if not a volunteer)
- Auction software (if you're using it)

Let me stop here for a second. Many of the costs I've just listed are usually paid to a third party such as a hotel or conference center. Early in the planning you'll discuss these with the site coordinator and be asked to sign a contract. Be sure you understand it.

Your contract will typically include: how many dinners are guaranteed and when you must provide the final tally of guests; whether you're offering a cash or open bar and whether there are corkage fees; is parking complimentary (e.g. validated).

If you don't understand every element of the contract you may be unpleasantly surprised at the end of the evening. I recommend you comb through it with your committee and make sure everyone agrees to all items.

Other miscellaneous expenses you might incur include:

- Printing
- Flyers
- Programs
- Signs and banners
- Catalogs
- Auction paddles
- Labels (name tags, bar codes)
- Postage (solicitation letters, thank you letter, mailing flyers)

- License fees (if appropriate)
- Tables, table skirts, chairs and lecterns
- Decorations
- Easels for displaying seating charts, directions, gifts
- Refreshments (if you are providing)
- Beer, wine, soda, bottled water
- Cups/glasses (beer and wine)
- Liquor and mixers (if appropriate)
- Coolers
- Ice
- Trash cans/bags
- Packing material (boxes, bubble wrap, peanuts)
- Raffle tickets

Once you've estimated all of your expenses, you're ready to calculate the cost of admission. I recommend that any costs associated with the location, dinner, auctioneer, and refreshments be included in the cost of admission. That way, all the money from auction bids and raffles goes to your organization. You never want to find yourself in a situation where you have to sell various items just to cover your costs.

You'll find a sample financial statement in Appendix Q.

5

Publicity

"What kills the skunk is the publicity it gives itself," observed Abraham Lincoln.

True enough, but if you want a killer auction, you're going to need all the attention you can get. And hopefully it'll be low cost or free.

If you'll be drawing most of your guests from within the organization, it's easy to minimize your costs. But if you need to attract guests from the community at large, then your costs will be higher.

■ Flyers

Flyers are probably the least expensive way to publicize your auction if most of your guests will be drawn from your own constituency. If your organization meets frequently or has a way to easily distribute information to those who might want to attend, then you're in luck. If not, you'll have to rely on mail, a much costlier alternative.

Send your flyers or letters out early – three months in advance for the first one, and a month prior for the second one. If RSVPs appear to be coming in slow, you might consider sending out a third.

When designing your flyer, make sure you include each of the following elements:

- Who your organization is
- Where and when the auction will be held
- How much it costs to attend
- A sampling of the items that will be auctioned
- A request to RSVP by a certain date
- It's going to be fun ... let them know!

■ Email

Another publicity option is to email potential guests, assuming these people have provided you with their email addresses. If you do use email, don't send attachments. By and large, individuals don't trust email attachments and for good reason – they're how most computer viruses are spread. Instead, create an email that looks similar to a flyer, using HTML (Hyper Text Format Language), and simply paste it into the body of your email. Chances are you have someone in your organization that understands HTML and can easily do this for you.

■ Commercial advertising

If your guests are members of the general community, and not necessarily members of your organization, reaching them will be more costly. But there are various ways to obtain free advertising. Try to get listed in the "community calendar" section of your local paper. Radio stations and sometimes TV stations have similar community service announcements.

Occasionally, media outlets will conduct an interview, which gives you an in-person opportunity to explain your event and talk up some of the unique items to be auctioned. Also, don't overlook the simple – putting a sign in front of your organization's headquarters, provided there are no zoning restrictions.

A week before their monthly bingo night, my local Knights of Columbus has a large banner hung up on the front of their building, which happens to be on a busy street. Also, the local catholic school puts up a sign announcing the annual charity auction as the date nears.

One last word about signs, or rather, billboards in this case. It's common to spot billboards around town that say: "Advertise Here." When you see one, give the company a call. It's not unusual for them to run your message for free (assuming you pay for the cost of the materials).

■ Invitations

If you're lucky enough to have a database of your members or guests from previous auctions, then you can send out formal invitations. The elements you need to include in your invitation are the same as those listed above for flyers. Again, mail these approximately 90 days before your event. It's also a good idea to send out periodic reminders to those who haven't sent in their RSVP.

6

The Timeline

"I love deadlines. I like the whooshing sound they make as they fly by." Some British comic said that, I think.

But, alas, developing a schedule at the very start of your auction planning is a must. By identifying the major decisions you must make, and when, and by allowing your various committees to lay out their own individual milestones, you can prevent real problems later.

In many ways, the final schedule itself isn't nearly as important as the brainstorming that'll go into its creation. Some of the best ideas will be generated this way.

■ When should we start?

As discussed earlier, most auction committees begin planning a full year in advance. Do yourself a big favor: even if you're a high-powered CEO with formidable management skills, do not underestimate the time required.

A sample schedule appears on the next two pages. This will help you flesh out the events that'll be necessary for your auction. It is just a starting point and you'll want to supplement and modify it as you see fit.

Sample Timeline
November to November

By early November	Obtain board approval
December to November	Committee status meetings
Mid-December	December status meeting
By mid-January	Recruit volunteers Hold planning meeting (with committee chairs) Identify auctioneer Contract with caterer Contract with photographer Train volunteer committees Mid-January status meeting
Late Jan. to mid-Oct.	Begin acquisition campaign Thank you letters mailed
Late January	First publicity mailing
Mid-February	February status meeting
Mid-March	March status meeting
Mid-April	April status meeting
Late May	May status meeting Mail invitations Second publicity mailing
Mid-June	June status meeting

Mid-June to mid-Oct	Begin receiving RSVPs
Mid-July	July status meeting Third publicity mailing
Mid-August	August status meeting Begin delineating between silent and live auction gifts Fourth publicity mailing
Mid-September	September status meeting
Mid-October	October status meeting
Late October	Print program Do dry run of auction Develop script for MC
Early November	November status meeting
Auction day	Set up room in morning Hold auction
Mid-November	Complete financial report
Late November	Conduct wrap-up meeting

7

How It All Works

"There are no extra pieces in the universe," says Deepak Chopra. "Everyone is here because he or she has a place to fill, and every piece must fit itself into the big jigsaw puzzle."

While an auction isn't metaphysical (good thing or I'd be lost), still there are many pieces to consider such as acquiring, cataloguing, and pricing items. How I suggest you approach these tasks is the subject of this chapter. Of course you'll need to adjust your way of doing things based on the size of your auction, the number of volunteers at your disposal, or the computer expertise on your team.

This guide presents a paper-based approach to auctions, but the processes can be performed using several commercially available auction software programs. In either case, the processes are essentially the same.

■ Acquisition

Acquisition is the process of securing gifts and completing the paperwork donors need to document the transaction. Acquisition also includes storing and pricing the gifts, and deciding whether you'll sell them in the silent or live auction.

• *Committee training*

It's important to hold an initial training session with volunteers involved in the acquisition process. First, this assignment can be daunting and the more prepared your volunteers are, the more at ease they'll be. Second, your committee must keep accurate records. This is to ensure you don't lose any gifts and that all parties involved have the documentation they need if audited by the Internal Revenue Service.

• *Working in teams*

Teams provide the moral support needed to approach a potential donor. Needless to say, when pairing people pay attention to personal dynamics. Chances are you have some in your organization who are very good at asking. You'll want to pair these folks with team members who are more reluctant. This also allows teams to share the workload, i.e. the more reserved person can take on tasks more suited to him or her (such as documentation and collection of the gifts).

• *Whom to approach for gifts*

Most of your gifts will come from local businesses or individuals within your organization (parents, members, patrons, parishioners). Local businesses will typically give for two reasons. First, as a gesture of good will to their community; second, because you're offering a bit of publicity. And of course your constituency will give (you hope) because they believe in your mission.

TIP: If you live in a community with local luminaries (a newscaster, radio personality, or sports figure, for example), approach them for a gift. It might be a dinner together, a tour, or a signed piece of memorabilia.

• *Start with last year's list*
If this isn't your organization's first auction, you're in luck. Last year's donor list contains people who, if they were thanked properly, will often give again. Have your committee review the list and divide the donors so they can be approached as soon as possible. As volunteers become more comfortable asking, they should be encouraged to approach new businesses as well.

• *First auction?*
If this is your first auction, don't despair. By brainstorming the businesses located in your community, as well as companies and individuals known to members of your auction committee, you can put together a pretty solid list of potential donors.

Be sure to focus your efforts on businesses that have the types of items you want to feature. Reviewing the index in your local yellow pages is a good strategy for finding the kind of gifts you'd like to secure.

• *Donations vs. gift certificates*
Many businesses, especially restaurants, will offer gift certificates. Accept these graciously, of course, but train your focus on companies that can donate tangible items. I recommend this for two reasons. First, tangible gifts create an exciting environment (imagine an auction with no actual gifts, just a slew of gift certificates). Second, a gift certificate will only bring in its face value, sometimes not even that.

On the other hand, a tangible gift is more likely to exceed its actual value.

• *Soliciting donations in person*

There are different ways to solicit donations from businesses but the most successful is by visiting the owner or manager in person. It's very difficult to turn away a volunteer who's standing right before you. This doesn't mean your first contact with the business should come as a surprise to the owner. To pave the way, some organizations mail a fact sheet about their auction prior to a volunteer visiting. You may also need to set up an appointment if the owner is seldom on the premises.

Also, when you're offered a gift, remember to obtain a business card and any other information you'll need to create the advertising copy for your program.

■ The acquisition process has two paths

Path 1 involves asking for the contribution, providing the donor with a receipt, accepting the item (tangible or intangible), ensuring that it's safely stored and eventually transported to the auction.

Path 2 involves recording each item, updating the auction catalog, deciding which auction the item will be placed in (silent or live), determining the item's value (to establish a minimum bid), and listing the item in the auction catalog.

The diagram on the next page shows the acquisition process and can be useful for training volunteers.

The Two Parallel Paths of Acquiring Gifts

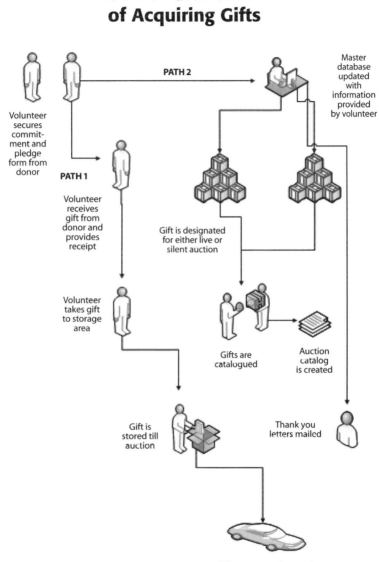

Volunteer secures commitment and pledge form from donor

PATH 2

PATH 1

Master database updated with information provided by volunteer

Volunteer receives gift from donor and provides receipt

Gift is designated for either live or silent auction

Volunteer takes gift to storage area

Gifts are catalogued

Auction catalog is created

Gift is stored till auction

Thank you letters mailed

Gifts transported to auction

8

The Auction Catalog

"I can resist everything except temptation," said Oscar Wilde, and people like him are just who you want to attract to your auction.

Every one of the tempting items you solicit must be catalogued. This is true for two reasons. First, you need to keep track of everything to calculate your profits, determine who your donors are (especially useful for future years), and satisfy the IRS if your organization is audited.

Second, you'll need to produce the Auction Program, which contains a listing of all of the items to be auctioned. Whether you use a spreadsheet or ledger book, you'll need to capture the following information:

1. **Item number:** A unique number assigned to each donation. This number cannot change even when an item is pulled from the auction.

2. **Item description:** Be as descriptive as possible here.

3. **Donated by:** List the name of the company or the individual making the donation.

4. **Item category:** The area of the auction where this item will appear (e.g. Health, Beauty and Fitness, Services, For the Home).

5. **Item special terms and conditions:** If a donation comes with any special conditions (a car with a minimum bid, for example, or a hotel stay with blackout dates) these must be captured here. You'll also list this information in the program so that the bidder has full-disclosure. It's also a good idea to have the auctioneer read the conditions before starting the bidding. In the silent auction, these conditions should be listed on the top of the bid sheet.

6. **Point of contact:** List the name of the person who's knowledgeable about the item should there be any questions.

7. **Point of contact title:** Manager, owner, or other appropriate title.

8. **Point of contact address**

9. **Point of contact phone**

10. **Point of contact email**

11. **Value:** This is the value assigned by the organization or by the person making the donation. It's important that you obtain this information, as it will be used to establish the "fair market value" (see Taxes in the Appendix).

12. **Date:** The date the donation was made.

13. **Gift Certificate:** Indicate if the donation is a gift certificate.

14. **Donation Taken By:** The person who obtained the donation.

15. **Storage Location:** Where the donation is being stored.

Note: At some point, usually two to three weeks prior to the auction to allow sufficient printing time, you'll need to complete your Auction Catalog. But anyone who's ever worked an auction knows that some of the best gifts take a long time to secure. Handle these late arriving gifts by producing an addendum that you photocopy and insert in the program.

TIP: Consider mailing an advance copy of your Auction Catalog to those who have RSVP'd. Another option is to post the catalog on your website and email the link to prospective attendees.

9

The Auction Program

Someone once said, "A road map always tells you everything except how to refold it."

Here's hoping your auction program eliminates that problem ... with staples.

Handed to attendees when they check in, your auction program is a road map for the evening. It contains a list of the evening's events and times, the rules of the auction, the names of those responsible for the event, a listing of all the items to be auctioned, and the advertisements of those companies that donated gifts to the auction.

■ Simple to Sophisticated

Programs can range from very simple to highly sophisticated, and the costs associated with producing them can vary accordingly.

This component of your auction is so important that typically a separate committee or person is solely dedicated to developing the program. Also, be aware that printing an auction program can be expensive. If yours is simple, perhaps it can be run off on a copy machine. But if you desire something more polished, make every attempt to have a local business pick up the printing costs.

■ Elements of the Auction Program

What follows below is a list of the components and sections that normally appear in an Auction program.

1) Cover
2) Front Page with invitation, theme, and date/place (this may be your cover)
3) Thank you to volunteers
4) Program
5) Menu or list of refreshments
6) List of benefactors
7) List of contributors
8) Auction committee members
9) List of all volunteers
10) Auction rules (see sample in Appendix R)
    a) General
    b) Live
    c) Silent
11) Live auction catalog section
12) Silent auction catalog section
13) Sponsor and donor advertisements (could be disbursed throughout)
14) Back cover (if necessary)

■ Imaginative descriptions

Your program should include creative write-ups to market your items. For example:

101 Paintball Magic

Have a ball. A paintball that is! Be the proud owner of a brand new high-powered paintball gun and all the accessories. Not only will you be well armed, you'll be well served with a package of 10 free passes to "Wally's Paintgun Park."

103 A Holy Feast

Father Chuck and his staff (Who knew they could cook?!) will bring a full-course spaghetti dinner for eight to your home. This package includes the finest spaghetti sauce known to Italians – a special secret recipe passed down to Father Chuck from his beloved mother. The dinner comes complete with salad, pasta, dessert, and of course fine Italian wine. Don't let your parish neighbors outbid you – you'll be sorry.

106 Gone Fishin'

Calling all anglers and angler wannabes. Enjoy a full day of offshore fishing on Peter Laduka's private fishing yacht. The trip will put out at the Charleston City Marina and will head for open ocean. Let the Captain and the Crew take your party of up to eight out to where the "big ones run." If you're lucky enough to catch a keeper, the crew will clean and package your prize.

TIP: Whatever form your Auction Catalog takes, be sure you back up your data frequently. If your catalog is kept in a manual ledger (paper), periodically make copies and safely store the material. If your data is electronic, make frequent backups and store on a USB stick or external drive.

10

Checking In

"People count up the faults of those who keep them waiting," says the French proverb. Always keep those words in mind when developing your auction's check-in procedures.

Checking in guests is fairly simple and consists of the following steps.

1) The guests arrive and approach the table displaying the letter of their last name.

2) The committee member at the table locates the guests' auction packet (from a box of packets stored alphabetically).

3) If they've already paid, the volunteer notes this on the attendance list and hands them their auction packet.

4) If they've submitted their RSVP but haven't paid, the volunteer collects the admission fee, marks them paid, and hands them an auction packet.

5) If a seating chart is used, the committee member directs them to the easel where the seating chart is located. If the auction is very large, it's advisable to have someone at the seating chart to help guests locate their seats.

■ Splitting up the Lines

To increase the efficiency of the check-in process, you'll want multiple lines. This can be done easily by placing signs in front of the check-in stations which show your guests in which line to stand based on their last names (A-L and M-Z, or A-H, I-Q and R-Z).

■ Auction packets

Each couple (or guest if attending alone) will be given a packet. This packet typically contains the following:

- Auction program
- Addendum to auction catalog (includes items submitted after the auction program was printed)
- Organization fact sheet
- Auction rules
- Payment options (checks, cash, credit cards)
- Advertising (some businesses may desire to provide your guests with coupons/flyers/ brochures)
- Silent auction closing time
- Drink coupons (if used)
- Raffle tickets (if used)
- Flyers for other upcoming events
- Auction paddles (two per couple with the same number printed on each).

See Appendix R for a sample auction program.

11

The Silent Auction

Once your guests check in, they'll socialize around the tables containing your silent auction items. You'll want to present these items in the most attractive light, as this will generate greater interest and lead to higher profits.

■ Silent Auction Categories

Arrange your items by categories using the same category numbering established in the acquisition phase. Here's an example.

SILENT AUCTION CATALOG INDEX

Catalog No.	Category
100's	Health, Beauty and Fitness
200's	Household
300's	Personal
400's	Getaways
500's	Gift Baskets
600's	Dinner +
700's	Sporting Goods
800's	Services

■ Silent auction table setup

Because you'll be arranging your silent auction items in categories, longer tables generally work best. Also, longer tables give buyers a sense that there's a flow of movement expected. This can prevent guests who are socializing from blocking a group of popular items.

Areas should be clearly marked with the category names. Hanging signs from the ceiling, or using stands set on the tables, allows your categories to be seen over people's heads. Placing categories that aren't as popular or have few gifts in between other more popular categories will help them get more attention.

■ Gift display

Display your gifts in the best possible light. Decorating your tables with confetti, balloons, attractive flyers, and centerpieces are all good ways to do this. Elevate some gifts on covered boxes to give a three-dimensional look. Make sure your Decorating Committee and your Silent Auction Committee are working together early in the process on the general layout of the items and the decorating scheme.

Note: *Never* place actual gift certificates on the tables. They can be easily stolen or misplaced. Instead, use a flyer to describe what the gift certificate is for (the flyer will likely be more attractive than the gift certificate anyway). Your gift certificates – you're likely to have quite a few of them – should be kept at the checkout table. Purchasers will pick them up when they pay at the end of the night. Note, if you're using an automated system that tracks gifts by bar codes, gift certificates can be delivered by runners once the silent auction results are entered in the computer.

TIP: It's important with your silent auction to state and enforce a minimum raise amount. Otherwise, bidders who lose out to bidders who fail to follow the rules will protest (loudly). By having a volunteer circulate through the tables, he or she can spot this problem before it gets out of hand.

■ Bid sheets

Shown on the next page, bid sheets are what guests use to record their bids. To prevent people from bidding an amount less than your minimum bid, you may want to enter the minimum bid in the first line, but leave the "Bidder Name" line blank. If you're using an automated system with bar codes, bidders simply peel off the barcode from their sheet of stickers and place it on the bid sheet next to the amount of their bid.

■ Silent auction table closing

It's a good idea to announce the closing of the silent auction table at prescribed intervals, such as 15 minutes, 10 minutes, 5 minutes. This encourages bidders to enter their "best and final" offer. It's also helpful to close different sections of the silent auction at different times, to allow your volunteers time to pick up all the bid sheets quickly.

SILENT AUCTION BID SLIP

Item Name _____

[*Insert description and any special conditions*]

Item No. _____
Donated by _____
Minimum bid: $_____
Minimum raise: $_____

Bidder Name	Bidder No.	Bid Amount

- *Silent Auction Winners*

Not all silent auction bidders will know if they've won when the tables close, as they may be socializing when the bid sheets are picked up. Therefore, it's important to create a Silent Auction Winner's Board to post the names and paddle numbers of the winning bidders. A large display board (or several) placed on an easel works well. Once the bid sheets are collected and taken to the checkout table for recording, these sheets can then be used to record the winners on the board.

12

The Live Auction

Whether you've opted for a professional or volunteer auctioneer, you'll still want to make sure you've closely coordinated how the live auction part of the evening flows. Your ultimate success depends on it.

■ Getting bidders in the mood

One way to get bidders excited is to show them during the silent auction what they'll see in the live auction. An easy way to do this is to create a computer slide show, which can be run automatically in a loop during the silent auction with a projector and a large screen. You can also take gifts from the live auction and have volunteers parade them around the room or set them up on tables near the entrance to the main hall where the live auction takes place.

TIP: For non-tangible items such as getaways and celebrity dinners, it's a good idea to create attractive posters. First, place them around the room where the silent auction takes place. Then, shortly before the live auction starts, move these into the live auction area and use them to display the item up for bid.

■ Opening and minimum bids

As I've mentioned, you'll need to establish opening bids for each of your items. In some instances, especially with high value items, donors themselves may decide the minimum bid. This is often the case with automobiles, where the dealership donates the car at a reduced price. The agreement with the dealership is that if the minimum bid isn't met, the car is returned.

Excepting in cases where minimum bids aren't met, it's good to establish an "all items must go" policy. This relieves the committee from having to keep an item until the next auction, protects the donor from some embarrassment (albeit not all), and makes the auction more interesting. Bidders want to believe that they have a chance to get the occasional item at a steal.

■ Room layout

Seating guests at round tables is usually the best option when you're serving a formal dinner. This creates an environment where groups can socialize and motivate each other to "go after" certain gifts. However, your silent auction should be conducted in a room where minimal seating is available. This prevents potential bidders from sitting with friends and never visiting the auction tables.

One scenario is to hold the auction in two adjacent rooms. The silent auction is held in the first, smaller room, and has rows of long tables to display the silent auction items.

Once the silent auction is finished, guests are then called into a larger room, such as a ballroom, and seated at large round tables (10 to 12 guests each) for dinner. Once dinner winds down, the live auction starts.

■ Live auction pace

The live auction must be fast-paced with few, if any, interruptions. The possible exception might be the announcements of door prize and raffle winners. Keeping the auction moving helps prevent guests from leaving. Any disruptions will create a good excuse for some guests to head for the door as everyone wants to avoid the notoriously long checkout lines.

■ Number of items to offer in the live auction

This really depends on whether you're using an amateur or professional auctioneer. To give you a rough idea, if the live auction is to last through the course of a dinner, and a professional auctioneer is used, 35 items is about the maximum. If you're using a volunteer auctioneer, the number should be closer to 20.

To warm up the audience, start with your more attractive but lower cost items. Then stagger the good items throughout the evening, saving your best and most enticing gifts for last. Your goal should be to create an item order that prevents your guests from leaving before the live auction is finished.

■ Paddles and the parading of items

Bidders will be given either paddles with a unique number (usually one number per couple) or the number will be printed on the back of the Auction Program itself.

In either case, when people bid, they raise their paddle or program in the air for the auctioneer or spotter to see.

■ The Bidding Process

The bidding process is fairly simple, but because the pace can be fast, some of your guests may feel intimidated. If you're using a professional auctioneer, make sure he or she understands your audience and goes slow in the beginning.

Perhaps you remember as I do the first time you attended an auction. You were probably a bit anxious and afraid of making a mistake. It took you a while to get used to the auctioneer's cadence. This will be the same for many in your audience. Expect them to be nervous at first. Good auctioneers know this. If you're using a volunteer auctioneer, you probably won't have to worry because things will be more casual.

■ Spotters

A couple of volunteers called spotters should be located on both sides of the room to assist the auctioneer in identifying bidders as their paddles are raised. Some bidders won't raise their paddles high enough. Consequently, spotters need to watch closely.

Early in the bidding, it can be a bit frantic and spotters can be a great help, especially to a volunteer auctioneer. Also, if working in a dark room, it can help if the spotters have flashlights to assist the auctioneer in determining who is bidding.

■ Recording the bidding

Three things that typically go wrong with live auctions are:
- The wrong bidder is documented as the winner
- The wrong winning bid amount is documented
- The invoice is misplaced

What happens is that the checkout process comes to a complete stop because invoices and certificates are misplaced. No one likes to stand in line and things can be ugly pretty quickly.

You can prevent these problems by following this simple process.

1) Two individuals should separately record the winning bidder's number and the winning bid. They should sit apart from each other and not communicate. One is called the "lead recorder" and the other is called the "backup recorder."

2) The invoices for each item should be organized in a stack in the same order in which items are auctioned. This should also be the same order in which items are numbered in your catalog.

3) The invoice should be printed on multi-part carbonless forms so that one copy is given to the winning bidder, while the original (top copy) is kept for the official auction records. Once the lead recorder fills out the invoices with the winning bidder's number and the amount, the invoice is taken to the backup recorder's table, validated, and then delivered to the checkout table and held for checkout later in the evening.

4) Once a winning bidder has been determined, the auctioneer should clearly finalize the sale by *slowly*

saying something to the effect: "Item number G137, a beautiful set of pearl ear rings, goes to bidder number 540 for a price of $450." It's amazing how easily a recorder can hear this and transpose the numbers (e.g. bidder number 450 for the price of $540). To prevent this, the lead recorder should repeat back to the auctioneer what was said. Once this repeat back is complete, then the lead recorder can then record this information on the invoice.

5) Periodically, and as discussed earlier, runners move the invoice from the lead recorders table to the checkout table (every five items or so). However, they must stop at the backup recorders table first to validate that the invoices agree. This way, if a discrepancy is noted, not too much time will have elapsed and the matter can quickly be resolved.

6) It is possible to lose invoices. If this were to happen, the backup recorder would have a record of the sale and a new invoice could be created based on the information recorded in the backup recorder's marked-up catalog.

7) If a discrepancy is noted during the validation process, the auction chair should work with all parties to resolve the problem immediately.

•••

The diagram on the next page shows how the bid recording process works. It's a good idea to share this with your volunteers so that they have a clear understanding of the role they play.

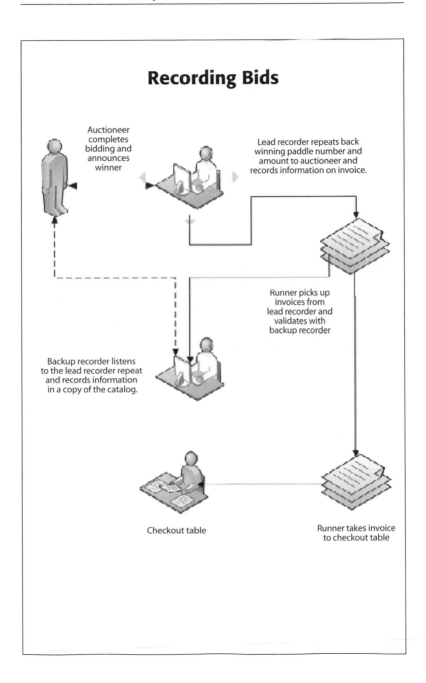

Lastly, remember that under your Live Auction Rules, "In the event of any dispute between bidders, the auctioneer shall have sole and final discretion to determine the successful bidder." If you're following the steps outlined above, disputes will be few and easy to resolve.

■ Checkout

Once the live auction is finished, everyone will want to checkout immediately. The night is late, many of your guests are tired, and the babysitter's on the clock. Because the process can be somewhat complicated, your team must fully understand all elements of the process beforehand, or confusion can quickly set in. By studying this next section carefully, talking it through with your team, and rehearsing this part of the event, you can ensure the checkout goes smoothly.

• Volunteers

You're going to need plenty of volunteers to conduct the checkout process. Thankfully, except for the cleanup crew, most of your committees will be free to assist. You'll need volunteers to process invoices, take payment, retrieve gifts, bag items, and yes, occasionally resolve disputes.

• Automated Checkout

The checkout process, like many other auction processes, can be automated. There are several database applications to choose from. However, technology can be fraught with problems. I recommend you use a manual process if this is your first auction, if your team isn't technically savvy, or if your auction is small.

If you're using an automated application, make sure you can quickly implement a manual process if something goes wrong. Think through ahead of time how you could recover manually. Have multiple hard copies of all of your database reports (invoices, receipts, auction item lists) on hand.

Lastly, if you're using an automated software program, try to have the individuals entering data located near the checkout tables (possibly in an adjoining room) but not in plain view. It can be difficult for these individuals to do what they need to do accurately and quickly if they're disturbed by the events going on around them. However, they need to be near the checkout table to answer questions that may arise.

■ Two manual checkout approaches

There are two manual approaches you can use. The first is a single stage checkout. This is done by organizing your stations by paddle numbers. The second approach is an assembly line checkout, where individual stations are used to conduct distinct processes (such as picking up of the invoice, making payment, and picking up the gift).

For auctions where the number of attendees exceeds 100, or if you have a limited number of volunteers, I suggest using the assembly line approach. This means your volunteers only need to understand a single component of the process. By doing that component over and over, they become more efficient at it. Another variation of this approach, which should be considered for very large auctions, is to create multiple instances of the "assembly lines" to prevent one very long line. Let's look at both processes in more detail.

• *Single Stage Checkout Process*

Here is a rough estimate of the number of stations you need if you're conducting a small auction:
• 100 attendees = 4 stations (paddle numbers 1-25, 26-50, 51-75, 76-100)
• 200 attendees = 8 stations
• 500 attendees = 20 stations

These estimates assume you can conduct one complete customer checkout in just over 2.5 minutes. Some checkouts will go faster, and some will go slower.

The basic functions each individual will need to perform are shown below.

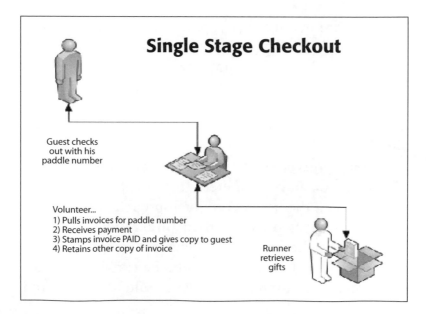

Single Stage Checkout

Guest checks out with his paddle number

Volunteer...
1) Pulls invoices for paddle number
2) Receives payment
3) Stamps invoice PAID and gives copy to guest
4) Retains other copy of invoice

Runner retrieves gifts

• *Assembly Line Checkout*

With this approach, you have four stations that guests pass through (shown on the next page). At the first station, the guest picks up the invoice which shows the total amount due. Invoices are organized by paddle number.

At the second or third stations as appropriate, guests either write a check/pay cash, or present a credit card. Once they've paid, the volunteer stamps both copies of their invoice (best to use a stamp to prevent someone from writing "paid" themselves). The guest then proceeds to the fourth station to present their invoice and receive the gift. Runners will be needed to retrieve the item.

For each "assembly line" instance you create, you'll need approximately five to six volunteers. One simple way to determine how many assembly lines to create is to take your total volunteers available and divide by 6. If you use multiple assembly lines, each assembly line will be devoted to a certain series of paddle numbers (1-100, 101-200, 202-300).

• *Advance Checkout*

Some guests will want to stay through the silent auction and then checkout before the live auction begins. You should have one checkout station open to take care of these guests.

Assembly Line Checkout

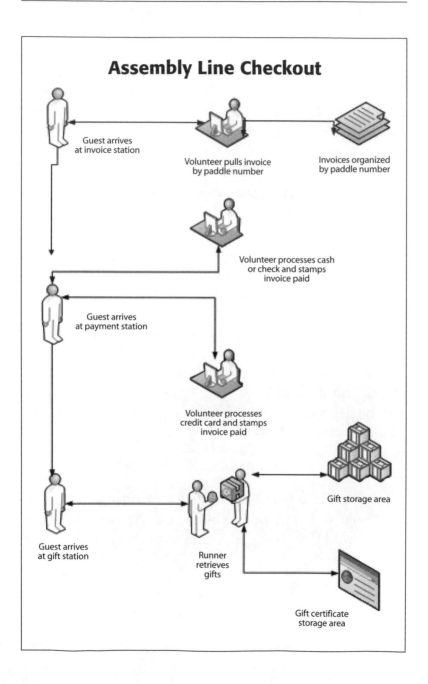

Guest arrives at invoice station

Volunteer pulls invoice by paddle number

Invoices organized by paddle number

Volunteer processes cash or check and stamps invoice paid

Guest arrives at payment station

Volunteer processes credit card and stamps invoice paid

Gift storage area

Guest arrives at gift station

Runner retrieves gifts

Gift certificate storage area

13

Additional Revenue Sources

"If opportunity doesn't knock, build a door," said Milton Berle. He could have been talking about auctions.

While most of your revenue will come from the sale of gifts, you can substantially increase your take by creating other opportunities for people to contribute.

■ Admission Fees

Most charity auctions charge an admission fee. Asking people to pay in advance helps to assure that those who say they're coming do in fact show up. How much you charge depends on the affluence of constituency, but since guests will be paying for auction items as well, admission shouldn't be steep.

If you can cover all your miscellaneous costs (paper products, office supplies, refreshments, cocktails) through admission fees, then the amount you receive from the sale of gifts will be pure profit.

■ Beer, Wine and Cocktails

If you decide to serve alcoholic beverages, you have several options for pricing. You can include all, some, or none of the costs in your admission.

If you want to include refreshments in your admission fee, you can issue drink tickets. Once the tickets are used, guests can purchase additional drinks with cash. The drink tickets given to the bartender help determine the number of drinks that were served (along with the cash that was received).

If you decide to serve cocktails in addition to wine and beer, you'll probably want to hire professional bartenders (with wine and beer you can often get by with volunteers). If you do ...

1) Make sure you check references and experience. This is especially important if they'll be accepting cash.

2) Sign a contract and make sure you understand the terms.

3) Ask about corkage fees, unsold bottles, and returns. If you're paying by the bottle, count the empty bottles.

4) Discuss how bartenders will dress to make sure it's appropriate for your event.

5) Discuss setup requirements such as tables and portable bars.

6) Lastly, check with your local liquor commission to ensure you have the appropriate licenses to serve whatever alcoholic beverages you've decided upon.

■ Raffles

Many auctions supplement their income by conducting raffles. But check with your local government to confirm that a raffle is legal in your area (there might well be restrictions).

The types of items you can raffle include just about anything: gift baskets, gift certificates, money, and even the centerpieces. Unlike door prizes (discussed later), raffle items should be desirable items bidders can view in advance (volunteers who enjoy socializing can carry around the items during the silent auction so that guests can see what they're attempting to win).

The drawings for raffle items should be held either before or during the live auction. If you believe some guests may leave prior to the drawing, you have a couple of options. You can let guests know in advance that they'll need to be present to win. Or you can use tickets that require guests to write their name on both parts and then contact them the next day.

TIP: The ticket rolls that contain two tickets with the same number (one ticket above and one below, with a perforation in between) are perfect for raffles. These are available at most office supply stores. Needless to say, if you're using tickets for other parts of your auction (e.g. drink tickets and door prizes), make sure to use different colored tickets for each purpose.

■ Door Prizes

If you have too many silent auction items, or items

you don't think will do well, then using them as door prizes is a good way to supplement your profit. Unlike raffle items, door prizes are generally a surprise. Tickets are sold throughout the silent auction and the drawing is held during the silent or live auction. Normally, a few door prize tickets are included in the price of admission and are contained in the auction packet.

■ Advertising

Another popular way to increase your revenue is to allow donors to advertise in your Auction Program, or allow them to provide flyers or coupons in the auction packet. Selling spots in your program can help local businesses become better known. The best time to do this is when you're meeting with them to ask for a gift.

TIP: A popular approach for securing advertising is to sell business card spots. This eliminates the need for a designer and makes the process easy enough to be attractive to the potential advertiser.

14

The Big Night

Muhammad Ali said it best: "I run on the road, long before I dance under the lights." And, fortunately, that's what you've done for the past 12 months.

The big night is finally here and all your planning and preparation is about to pay off. But you're not home free yet. Here's where you have to train all your focus on logistical details. You don't want something as simple as the sound system failing to completely sabotage your event.

And speaking of unexpected problems, and the need for contingency plans, consider what you'd do if:

• Your auctioneer comes down with laryngitis

• Two silent auction bidders get into a heated argument over an item

• The fire department decides to have a fire alarm test

• You're using an automated check-out system and lose your Internet connection

I recently attended an auction where a number of guests arrived who hadn't registered. A simple thing, but a potential headache. Fortunately, the committee had planned for this and had extra packets and bidding information (numbers, paddles) available. They also made sure the caterer could accommodate a certain number of additional guests if it proved necessary. More importantly, they had trained the auction check-in staff on what to do if this happened.

■ Auction night crew

On event night, each of your volunteers must clearly understand their role. They must also know who to turn to if they need assistance. For this reason, it's a good idea one or two nights prior to the event to do a "walk through" or "dress rehearsal." You might even appoint a "devil's advocate" and have that individual imagine the things that could go wrong.

■ Setup

If possible, the room should be set up the day before the auction, with the exception of placing the gifts on the silent auction table. It is possible to set up with the gifts in place, but if you do, you'll need a security guard. A better plan is to bring the gifts the morning of the auction and have volunteers throughout the day make sure nothing "walks away." Silent auction gift certificates should always be safeguarded and never displayed until they're paid for by the guest.

■ Checklists

To help you avoid glitches, I'm including the following checklists in Appendix P:
  • Room set-up

- Refreshments
- Audio-visual equipment
- Check-in and check-out
- Raffle and door prizes
- Silent auction
- Live auction
- Cleanup

■ Accepting and safeguarding your guests' money

Most of us don't carry around wads of cash. We rely instead on our local ATMs and especially our credit card.

When it comes to auctions, a frequent question I'm asked is, "Should we accept credit cards?"

It's possible to run an auction without taking credit cards – as long as you announce it early and remind your guests before they arrive. But accepting MasterCard, Visa or American Express is a tremendous convenience to your guests and it will boost your returns.

If you decide to take credit cards, your organization will need a "merchant account." You can arrange for this through your bank or credit union, provided your organization is "brick and mortar" (you have a physical site where you conduct business). Chances are your organization already has a merchant account. If so, check with the appropriate person to ensure you understand the procedures that'll be required on auction night.

■ Night of the auction deposit and security

At the close of the evening you'll need to ensure that your cash, credit card slips, and checks are safeguarded and safely deposited. All collections should be verified by multiple parties and there should be two-person control over the money until all proceeds are deposited.

Depending on the amount of money your auction generates, you might want to enlist the services of a security firm or security officer to help move the money from the auction site to wherever it will be deposited that evening.

■ Reporting

Remember, you'll need to report your auction results to the organization's financial officer. Make sure you keep all receipts and records.

16

Auction Software and Online Auctions

Perhaps you agree with Dale Dauten when he says, "It's time to re-appreciate the original software: paper."

As a technology enthusiast I don't agree, but I can appreciate the sentiment, especially when a new software program I've just installed freezes up.

Nonetheless, there are good auction software packages available. And if you Google "auction software, silent auction software, or charity auction software" several will come up. When trying to identify the best program for you, keep the following tips in mind:

1) Ask the company how long it has have been in business and how many customers it has.

2) Ask for a list of references and call several.

3) Ask for a trial version of the software products that interest you. Most companies will oblige. If they don't, move on.

4) Find out how you'll be charged. Is it per event, a

commission of sales, are there annual maintenance fees?

5) Choose a system that will streamline the check-in and check-out processes. Remember, the weakest link in the entire auction process is "checkout."

6) Choose a system that tracks your donors *and* your attendees. These are your best prospects for both gifts and revenue.

7) Choose software that can produce invoices, programs, catalogs, bid sheets, name tags, gift certificates, and end-of-event financial reports that are easy to read and well-formatted.

8) Some systems are now web-based, and therefore don't require you to install the software on your own computer. This allows for multiple team members to access the system from anywhere to record gifts, donors, and other information. However, before you purchase a system that's web-based, discuss with the manufacturer what would happen if you lost connectivity on auction night.

■ Online Auctions

The focus of this book is on the "traditional" auction, where a group of people gather in a room and bid on selected items. Of course, in this age of the Internet, other options have sprung up, in particular, online or "virtual" auctions. Here, individuals bid on items simply with a click of their mouse.

Personally, I don't care for online auctions. And that

comes from someone who's very comfortable with and embraces technology. Granted, you don't have to worry about a slew of things: a physical location, decorating, refreshments, set-up -- you name it.

But an online auction simply doesn't offer the same opportunity for networking and fun that a traditional auction offers. Remember, a well-run charity auction is a social event. Often there's dinner, plenty of mingling, and much good-natured ribbing. Compare that to clicking a mouse in the confines of your den.

But more importantly, since this is a fundraising event, you won't raise nearly the same amount of money from an online auction. The synergy just isn't there.

Still, if you wish to pursue this option, there are various companies that will conduct the event for you. Again, simply Google "online auction companies" and plenty of options will appear.

A Last Word

Realizing that "Advice is like castor oil, easy to give, but dreadful to take," let me close with just a few tips I hope you'll heed:

• Start early. Successful auctions require at least 9 to 12 months to plan and execute.

• Delegate. If you're the chairperson of the entire event, or the chair of a subcommittee, you simply can't do it all yourself.

• Manage and massage your database. This list represents your best donors (those contributing items and those purchasing them). Add to your list each year and you'll grow a very profitable program over time.

• As the event gets closer, focus on checkout. This is where most auctions founder. Yours won't because you will have trained your staff and rehearsed the process two or three times before the big event.

Oh, and one more thing: have some fun. That's key.

Sure, there will be frustrations. And more than once you'll feel like slapping a fellow committee member with that auction paddle. But the rewards, psychological and financial, can be great. So can the memories.

Simply commit yourself to the task and follow the guidance, tips, and tricks I've laid out in this book. And remember what Vince Lombardi said: "The dictionary is the only place where success comes before work."

You're going to do great!

APPENDIX

A. Sample Agenda for Initial Meeting
B. Sample Auction Fact Sheet
C. Script for Calling Previous Donors
D. Script for Calling Prospective Donors
E. Contribution Agreement
F. Contribution Agreement For Quid Pro Quo Contributions
G. Sample Letter of Introduction
H. Sample Thank You Letter
I. Acquisition Tracking Sheet
J. Gift Ideas
K. Sample Auction Announcement
L. Sample Invitation
M. Auction Check-In Sheet
N. Silent Auction Bid Slip
O. Sample Auction Invoice
P. Checklists
Q. Sample Financial Statement
R. Sample Auction Program
S. Sample Thank You Letter To Committee Members
T. Door Prize Registration Slips
U. Taxes

SAMPLE AGENDA FOR INITIAL MEETING

The Hartsdale School Charity Auction

1. **Event schedule:**

   Indicate the date, time and location of this year's auction.

2. **Information about last year:**

   In discussing last year's auction, list the date the event was held, the location, total attendance, and the financial results broken down by revenue stream (as shown below):

Door Entry Fees:	$_____
Raffle:	$_____
Live Auction (# of items):	$_____
Silent Auction (# of items):	$_____
Expenses:	$_____
Total Profit:	$_____

3. **Live auction acquisition efforts for this year:**

   During this part of the agenda you'll want to discuss the various live auction gift ideas the Acquisition Committee should pursue. These may include: travel, dinners, VIP tours, dining at special locations, tickets to major sporting events, professional services, jewelry, vehicles, excursions, and the like.

4. **Silent Auction acquisition efforts for this year:**

   Here you'll discuss the type of items the Acquisition

Committee will try to secure for the silent auction. These might include: children's items, items for pets, gourmet food baskets, tickets to shows and sporting events, professional services such as babysitting, hairstyling, tutoring, training, travel, hotel stays, house and garden items, gift certificates.

5. **Acquisition strategy**

During this part of the meeting, you'll discuss the types of potential donors to approach. They might be large corporations, local businesses, mall chain stores, and other organizations and individuals within your organization.

6. **Acquisition process**

Here you'll identify potential donors to approach based on personal contacts, the scripts to be used for phone calls, and information about your organization that solicitors will find helpful to share with potential donors.

7. **Publicity**

Here you'll discuss what tactics and strategies you have for publicizing your auction.

8. **Logistics**

The logistics of planning and executing an auction can be daunting. As a result, it's imperative to discuss the various elements so that all volunteers understand how the pieces fit together. The elements you'll want to cover include the following.

- Tracking acquisitions
- Accounting responsibilities
- Auction check-in
- Auction check-out
- Raffle sales
- Assisting with the live auction
- Photography
- Decorations
- Food and beverage
- Publicity
- RSVPs
- Program
- Stage production and lighting

9. **Contact information for attendees**

Before adjourning the meeting, be certain you have everyone's contact information.

SAMPLE AUCTION FACT SHEET

An auction fact sheet is most often used when soliciting gifts. It gives volunteers the information they may need to explain the organization, its mission, and the details of the auction.

Event: The Hartsdale School Charity Auction

Beneficiary: Hartsdale School Scholarship Fund

Date: September 10, 20__

Location: Hartsdale School Gymnasium

Sponsors: The Friends of Hartsdale School

Background information on the sponsors: We're a nonprofit organization working to raise funds for various school programs, including annual scholarships. Currently we are 75 members strong.

Last year's auction results: Last year we awarded scholarships of $2,000.00 each to 25 deserving students. Our goal this year is to award at least the same number of scholarships.

Advertising opportunity: All donations will be featured in our program and acknowledged publicly during the auction to ensure that each donor is properly recognized.

Your gifts are tax deductible: The tax identification number of our organization is _____.

SCRIPT FOR CALLING PREVIOUS DONORS

Company name: _____

Company address: _____

Phone number: _____

Point of contact's name: _____

Email address: _____

Gift donated last year: _____

Call Log

Date call made: _____

Time call made: _____

Person spoken to: _____

Result of call: _____

Hello. My name is ____. May I speak with ____(the manager or head of marketing).

   If the manager IS present, SKIP this step.
   Otherwise ask as appropriate:

What is your managers name? _____

I see, do you know when he/she might be available?_____

Is this a good number to reach him/her?_____

Thank you for your help, I'll call back

Hello Mr./Ms. _____

My name is _____ *and I'm calling on behalf of* _____.
Last year you generously donated a gift for our Auction,
the proceeds of which go to the _____. *I'm calling to*
ask if you'd be willing to contribute again.

Wait and refer to the fact sheet if necessary.

Thank you Mr./Ms. _____

If appropriate: *We'll send out a confirmation letter in the*
next few weeks. The letter will give you the information
you need to make your donation. However, if you should
have any questions, please contact me. My name is
_____ *and my phone number is*_____. *You can also*
email me at _____.

Thank you again. Goodbye

SCRIPT FOR CALLING PROSPECTIVE DONORS

Company name: _____

Company address: _____

Phone number: _____

Point of contact's name: _____

Email address: _____

Call Log

Date call made: _____

Time call made: _____

Person spoken to: _____

Description of the call: _____

Hello. My name is _____ and I'd like to speak with _____ (the manager or head of marketing).

>If the manager IS present, SKIP this step.
>Otherwise, ask as appropriate

What is your managers name?_____

I see, do you know when he/she might be available?_____

Is this a good number to reach him/her?_____

Thank you for your help, I'll call back.

•••

Hello. My name is _____ and I'm calling on behalf of the _____. Were a nonprofit organization that raises funds for the _____.

I'm calling to ask if you'd be willing to donate a gift for our annual fundraising auction.

Not only will you be helping a great cause, but we'll feature you in our auction program and your generosity will be acknowledged during the event.

The attendance at last year's auction was _____. Will you consider a gift?

Wait and refer to the fact sheet if necessary.

Thank you Mr./Ms. _____

If appropriate: *We'll send out a confirmation letter in the next few weeks. The letter will give you the information you need to make your donation. However, if you should have any questions, please contact me. My name is _____ and my phone number is_____. You can also email me at _____.*

Thank you again. Goodbye

CONTRIBUTION AGREEMENT

You'll use this agreement to document each donation. A copy should also be given to the acquisition committee for accounting purposes. Additionally, this form contains the information you need to list the item in your auction program.

Organization Name & Address
Federal Tax ID#

Auction Contribution Agreement

_____ herby agrees to donate the item(s) or service(s) described below:

_____

_____

Estimated Value: $_____

Date:_____

Name: _____

Title: _____

Address: _____

Telephone: _____

Email Address: _____

Please retain a copy of this form for you records and to substantiate your contribution to a Federal tax-exempt organization.

Auction Committee Use Only:

Item Received:_____

Date Received:_____

Item Section Assigned:_____

Item Number:_____

CONTRIBUTION AGREEMENT
FOR QUID PRO QUO CONTRIBUTIONS

Occasionally a donor may receive something of value (say, a commemorative clock) in return for her gift. This is known as a "quid pro quo" donation and has particular tax consequences (see Appendix U section on "Taxes"). This agreement is used to document the donation and to provide the information your acquisition and finance committees need to properly account for the gift.

Organization Name & Address
Federal Tax ID#

Auction Contribution Agreement

_____herby agrees to donate the item(s) or service(s) described below:

_____

_____

Estimated Value of Donation: $_____
Date:_____

In exchange, the donor will receive:

Type of goods or services:_____
Estimate value of goods or services: $_____
Date:_____

Note: The amount of the contribution that is deductible for federal income tax purposes is limited to the excess of the amount of any money contributed

*by the donor over the value of the goods and services
furnished to the donor by the auction committee.*

Name: _____

Title: _____

Address: _____

Telephone: _____

Email Address: _____

> **Please retain a copy of this form for your records
> and to substantiate your contribution to a
> Federal tax-exempt organization.**

Auction committee use only:

Item received: _____

Date received: _____

Item section assigned: _____

Item number: _____

SAMPLE LETTER OF INTRODUCTION

Organization Letterhead

Date

Dear Mr./Ms. _____,

I am writing to ask for your support on behalf of the [*insert organization's name*]. We are a nonprofit organization that raises funds for [*insert organization's cause*].

Each year [*insert what the organization does*]

_____

_____

In a few days, I'll be calling to ask if you would consider making a gift to our annual fundraising auction to be held on [*insert date*]. You'll be helping a great cause and, in exchange for your donation, you'll be prominently featured in our program and acknowledged during the auction.

I look forward to speaking with you.

Sincerely,

[*Acquisition Committee Chairperson's Name*]

SAMPLE THANK YOU LETTER

Organization Letterhead

Date

Dear Mr./Ms. _____,

The [*insert organization's name*] would like to thank you for your support of our recent fundraising auction to benefit the [*insert organization's cause*].

I'm pleased to report that, owing in part to you, the auction was a huge success and we raised [*insert amount*].

As you know, you were listed in the auction program and your name was announced by the auctioneer at the start of the bidding of your item.

Thank you again for helping to further this great cause. We recognize and appreciate your support.

Sincerely,

[*Acquisition Committee Chairperson's Name*]

ACQUISITION TRACKING SHEET

Using your favorite spreadsheet program, create an Acquisition Tracking Sheet with the following columns:

❑ Item Number

❑ Point of Contact (POC) for Item

❑ POC Title

❑ POC Telephone

❑ POC Address

❑ POC Email

❑ Item Description

❑ Item Category

❑ Date Donated

❑ Donation Taken By

❑ Value

❑ Gift Certificate (Y/N)

❑ Restrictions on Gift

❑ Storage Location

GIFT IDEAS

LIVE AUCTION

- Round trip airline tickets
- Season tickets to a sporting event
- Dinner for eight given by someone in the organization
- Vacations
- Exotic (airfare, hotel, car)
- Local (Bed and breakfast)
- Professional portrait
- Dinner with someone important

- Fine jewelry (ring, bracelet)
- Automobile donated by dealership
- Homemade quilt
- Pool table, jukebox
- Reserved seats at organizational event
- Limo service for an evening
- Reserved parking
- Painting
- Sailing lessons
- Fishing excursion

SILENT AUCTION

Health, Beauty and Fitness

- Orthodontic treatment
- Dental hygienist visit
- Color analysis and makeover
- Haircut
- Skin products
- Salon visit
- Spa visit
- Nail care visit
- Personal trainer visit

- Hair products
- Pedicure
- Massage
- Membership with weight loss program
- Membership to fitness club
- Chiropractic visit

GIFT IDEAS (CONT'D)

Services

- Car servicing
- Wash
- Oil change
- Front end alignment
- Brake work
- Tire rotation
- Chimney sweep services
- Gutter cleaning
- Air conditioning maintenance
- Discount off security system installation
- Discounted new windows
- Handyman services
- Appliance repair
- Financial planning services
- Tax services
- Safe deposit box rental
- Settlement fees for a real estate transaction
- Computer consultation
- Resume preparation
- Typing services
- Bridge lessons
- Poker lessons
- Foreign language instruction
- Daycare services
- Maid service
- Drycleaning services
- Party planning
- Catering

For the Home

- Room makeover
- Decorating services
- Custom framing
- Landscaping services
- Crafts
- Household items
- Vase
- Frames
- Wreaths
- Bowls
- Ceramics
- Baskets
- Furniture
- Florist gift certificate
- Family photographs
- Paintings
- Scrapbook creation

GIFT IDEAS (CONT'D)

Personal

- Sunday brunch
- Jewelry
- Necklace
- Rings
- Earrings
- Pins
- Baskets filled with items
- Kitchen renovation
- Tea service
- Car care
- Beauty items
- Baby items
- Liquors
- Gift certificates
- Baby gifts

Sporting Goods

- Tickets to sporting events (college & professional)
- Football
- Basketball
- Baseball
- Soccer
- Hockey
- Memorabilia
- Golf lessons
- Tennis lessons
- Golf outings
- Golf club
- Ski vacations

Dinners +

- Restaurant gift certificates
- Brunch
- Lunch at the office
- Honey-baked hams
- Desserts
- Coffees
- Wine
- Catered party
- Donor hosted dinners

Getaways

- River cruises
- Private tours of local landmarks
- Lunch w/the mayor
- Ballet tickets
- Symphony tickets
- Trips to area hotspots
- Bed and breakfast weekends

GIFT IDEAS (CONT'D)

Baskets

- Gift wrapping items
- Pasta
- Mother's Day
- Father's Day
- Sport
- Seasonings
- Coffee and tea
- Wine
- Hawaiian
- Cooking
- Bath items
- Beauty items
- Tools
- Scrapbooking supplies
- Gardening

SAMPLE AUCTION ANNOUNCEMENT

The auction announcement will be used in your various promotions (e.g. bulletins, print media, flyers). Developing a standard announcement insures that all of your information is consistent and correct.

Welcome to the Hartsdale School Charity Auction

Date: Saturday, April 16, 20__

Time: 7:00 to 9:00 p.m. – Silent Auction
9:00 to 10:30 p.m. – Live Auction
10:30 to 11:00 p.m. – Checkout

Location: Hartsdale School Gymnasium
100 Main Street, Jackson, MI 49259

Guests: Encouraged

Attire: Informal

Price: $25 per person payable in advance

Mail Checks Payable to:
Hartsdale School, P.O. Box 123, Jackson, MI 49259

Menu: Beer, wine, soda and other beverages

RSVP   To Mrs. Smith at (317) 456-7895.

Parking: Ample parking in main lot.

Directions: Main Street is located at the intersection of Apple and Orange Meadow, just off Interstate 695.

APPENDIX K

SAMPLE INVITATION

You Are Invited to:

The Hartsdale School
Charity Auction
"Mardi Gras"

DATE: Saturday, April 16, 20__

TIME: 6:00 p.m. – 10:00 p.m.

Hartsdale School Gymnasium
100 Main Street, Jackson, MI 49259

ADMISSION: $25 per person in advance
or $30 per person at the door

RSVP by March 6 to Mrs. Jansen (307) 444-2424

or

Send check payable to:

Friends of the Hartsdale School to:
The Hartsdale School
100 Main Street
Jackson, MI 49259

All proceeds benefit
The Friends of Hartsdale School

AUCTION CHECK-IN SHEET

Guest/Paddle #	Guest Name	Address	Phone	Email	Arrived?	Amount Owed	Paid (Y/N)
001	Mr. John Smith	93 Main St Your City, MI 12345	(808) 555-1212	jsmith@ email.com	Y	0	N/A
002	Mrs. John Smith	93 Main St Your City, MI 12345	(808) 555-1212	msmith@ email.com	Y	0	N/A
003	Ms. Betty Nye	43 Elm St Your City, MI 12345	(616) 555-1212	bnye@ email.com		$15	N

SILENT AUCTION BID SLIP

Item Name _____

[_Insert description and any special conditions_]

Item No. _____

Donated by _____

Minimum bid: $_____

Minimum raise: $_____

Bidder Name	Bidder No.	Bid Amount

SAMPLE AUCTION INVOICE

Hartsdale School Charity Auction

Date of Auction: _____

Invoice Number: _____

Guest Name:

_____

Catalog # _____

Item Description:

_____

_____

Value: $ _____

Price Paid: $ _____

Make checks payable to:

The Hartsdale School
100 Main Street
Jackson, MI 49259

Thank you! Through your support, The Friends
of the Hartsdale School are able to provide
scholarships to those in need.

CHECKLISTS

Room Reservation

- Obtain a signed contract.
- When is the room available for setup?
- Who will be the room manager and will they be available throughout the night?
- Who is responsible for setup?
- Who is responsible for cleanup?
- What are the number and type of tables needed?
- How many chairs will be needed?
- Will a sound system be available?
- Will a podium or lectern be available?
- Will a portable stage be available?
- Are there any decoration restrictions?
- Who is responsible for catering?
- Are there any corkage fees (catered bar)?
- Are there any hidden costs (lighting and sound technicians)?
- Does the location have the appropriate licenses (liquor)?
- Is there a phone number parents can leave for babysitters?
- What if the auction runs late, are there any additional fees?
- If the auction does run late, is there an absolute time guests must be out of the room?

Room Setup

- Signs and banners
- Check-in/Check-out tables
- Silent auction tables

CHECKLISTS (CONT'D)

Room Setup *(continued)*

- Tables and chairs throughout room for socializing and placing drinks/deserts (not too many, you want people milling about bidding on items at the silent auction)
- Chairs for live-auction
- Lecterns for making announcement and for the auctioneer
- Sound system
- Portable bar or tables for bars
- Table skirts
- Decorations (consistent with theme)
- Secure room to store gifts
- Easels for displaying charts and gifts (non-tangible gifts)
- Movie screen if presentations are given
- Security guard or team of volunteers to ensure gift security before auction

Refreshments *(consider those that apply)*

- Confirm event with bartender/caterers 30 days and 7 days before the event
- Beer
- Wine
- Soda (diet and non-diet)
- Bottled water
- Cups/glasses (beer and wine)
- Liquor (if appropriate)
- Coolers
- Ice
- Trash cans/bags

CHECKLISTS (CONT'D)

Refreshments *(continued)*

- Mixers (if appropriate)
- Bottle openers
- Napkins
- Paper towels
- Change box and change

Sound System

- Sound system availability confirmed
- Sound system tested the day before the event
- Sound system tested the day of the event
- Microphones present
- Extension cords (if necessary)
- Acoustic levels set early in the day

Projection System

If you are using a projector to display gifts on a large screen to the guests during the silent auction or during the auction itself, you will need the following items.

- Computer (laptop most likely and a backup)
- Computer files with the actual presentation (and backup copies)
- Extension Cord
- Projector (extra bulb or backup projector)
- Movie screen (portable or fixed)

CHECKLISTS (CONT'D)

Check-in

- Check-in table(s)
- Table skirt
- Banners/signs
- Auction packets (discussed below)
- Cashbox(s) and cash to make change
- Seating chart (if appropriate)
- Calculators
- Pens

Checkout

- Cashbox
- Cash
- Sufficient change
- "Paid" Stamp (and ink pad if necessary)
- Credit card machine
- Credit card forms
- Phone Lines (to call in credit card verification)
- Calculators
- Bags
- Packing material (boxes, bubble wrap, peanuts, etc.)

Raffle and Door Prize

- Raffle Tickets
- Pens
- Drawing Jar
- Door prize and raffle gifts
- Baskets for carrying tickets and collecting money
- Change

CHECKLISTS (CONT'D)

Silent Auction

- Silent auction tables
- Table skirts
- Table decorations
- Bid sheets and backer sheets (colored)
- Pens (on strings or ribbons)
- Easel to display winning bid posters
- Posters to display winning bids
- Permanent markers

Live Auction

- An auctioneer
- Lectern
- Microphone
- Auctioneer cue cards or program with necessary information for every item to be auctioned
- Times that raffles or door prizes will be announced built into cue cards
- Easels or projection screen to display non-tangible gifts
- Poster for non-tangible gifts (if used)
- Volunteers to serve as spotters (with flashlights)
- Runners to retrieve, stage or display auction items

Auction cleanup

- Plenty of volunteers
- Access to cleaning supply rooms (Brooms, mops)
- Trash bags
- Empty boxes to carry away supplies

SAMPLE FINANCIAL STATEMENT

RECEIPTS

Admission	$1,125
Raffle	525
Live auction	6,040
Silent auction	6,589
Individual cash contributions	450
Miscellaneous	105
Total Receipts	$14,834

EXPENSES

Food	$950
Supplies	$357
Credit card fees	$360
Hall rental	$500
Printing	$375
Postage	$625
Total Expenses	$3,167

NET (profit/loss) $11,667

The Friends of the Hartsdale School Invites You to the 13th Annual Charity Auction "Mardi Gras"

Saturday, April 16, 20__
6:00 p.m.

Hartsdale School Gymnasium
100 Main Street, Jackson, MI 49259

*All proceeds benefit
the Friends of the Hartsdale School*

We would like to express our
deep appreciation to the hundreds of
volunteers and businesses who have made
this evening a reality.

We are touched by your generosity
and kindness.

Name of Chair or Co-Chairs

Auction Co-Chairs
20__

Evening's Program

6:00 p.m. – 7:30 p.m.
Cocktails, Silent Auction and
Viewing of All Auction Items

7:30 p.m.
Dinner

8:15 p.m.
Introductions

8:30 p.m. – 10:00 p.m.
Live Auction

Auction items may be paid for
anytime throughout the evening.

All items must be paid for
and picked up tonight.

DINNER MENU

Poached Norwegian Salmon with Fresh Dill
Spring Salad with Palm and Plum Tomato Vinaigrette

Filet Mignon
Fresh Cut Asparagus and Garlic Mashed
Red Potatoes

Or

Red Snapper
Summer Squash Medley
and a Bed of Jasmine Rice

Trio of Desserts
Blackberry Cheesecake
Assorted Fruit Tarts
White Chocolate Truffles in Strawberry Sauce

Coffee and Tea

BENEFACTORS

List Name, List Name, List Name, List Name, List Name,

List Name, List Name, List Name, List Name, List Name,

List Name, List Name, List Name, List Name, List Name,

List Name, List Name, List Name, List Name, List Name,

List Name, List Name, List Name, List Name, List Name,

List Name, List Name, List Name, List Name, List Name,

List Name, List Name, List Name, List Name, List Name,

List Name, List Name, List Name, List Name, List Name,

List Name, List Name, List Name, List Name, List Name,

List Name, List Name, List Name, List Name, List Name,

List Name, List Name, List Name, List Name, List Name,

List Name, List Name, List Name, List Name, List Name,

List Name, List Name, List Name, List Name, List Name.

SAMPLE AUCTION PROGRAM (CONT'D)

CONTRIBUTORS

List Name, List Name, List Name, List Name, List Name,

List Name, List Name, List Name, List Name, List Name,

List Name, List Name, List Name, List Name, List Name,

List Name, List Name, List Name, List Name, List Name,

List Name, List Name, List Name, List Name, List Name,

List Name, List Name, List Name, List Name, List Name,

List Name, List Name, List Name, List Name, List Name,

List Name, List Name, List Name, List Name, List Name,

List Name, List Name, List Name, List Name, List Name,

List Name, List Name, List Name, List Name, List Name,

List Name, List Name, List Name, List Name, List Name,

List Name, List Name, List Name, List Name, List Name,

List Name, List Name, List Name, List Name, List Name.

AUCTION COMMITTEE

List Name
List Name
Auction Co-Chairs

Acquisition List Names	*Advertising* List Names
Invitations/Check-in List Names	*Publicity* List Names
Catalog List Names	*Silent Auction* List Names
Live Auction List Names	*Miscellaneous Revenue* List Names
Auction Check-out List Names	*Volunteer Coordination* List Names
Thank You's List Names	*Finance* List Names

AUCTION VOLUNTEERS

List Name, List Name, List Name, List Name, List Name,

List Name, List Name, List Name, List Name, List Name,

List Name, List Name, List Name, List Name, List Name,

List Name, List Name, List Name, List Name, List Name,

List Name, List Name, List Name, List Name, List Name,

List Name, List Name, List Name, List Name, List Name,

List Name, List Name, List Name, List Name, List Name,

List Name, List Name, List Name, List Name, List Name,

List Name, List Name, List Name, List Name, List Name,

List Name, List Name, List Name, List Name, List Name.

If we have missed anyone, please accept
our apologies and let us know.
We would like to personally thank this individual.

AUCTION RULES
AND REGULATIONS

General Auction Rules

1. All sales are final. No exchanges or refunds are permitted. Everything is sold "as is". Please read specifications and limitations carefully. All items must be removed from the site on the night of the auction.

2. By his purchase, the buyer waives any claims for liability against either this organization or the donor of the property or services. Neither the organization nor the donor is responsible for any personal injuries or damages to property that may result from the use of the property or services sold.

3. Payment in full is mandatory for all auction items by the end of the evening of the auction. Cash, checks, VISA, MasterCard will be accepted. Items may be paid for individually or collectively at the end of the evening. After payment is made, a receipt will be issued by the cashier. This receipt is needed to claim items.

4. Bidder numbers will be issued at registration.

SAMPLE AUCTION PROGRAM (CONT'D)

After receipt of this number, each bidder is responsible for the use of the number throughout the evening.

5. Absentee bids cannot be accepted.

6. Check with your own tax advisor as to the deductibility of the purchase of each item.

Silent Auction Rules

1. All sales are final.

2. Winners will be posted as soon as possible after each section is closed.

3. Bidding will close by section.

4. Each Bid must have the name, auction number, and bid legibly printed.

5. You may bid as often as you like on each item.

6. You do not have to be present to win. Payment and pickup must occur within seven days from the close of the auction or the next bidder will be entitled to the item.

7. If the proper raise in price has not been adhered to, the previous bidder will be entitled to the item.

SAMPLE AUCTION PROGRAM (CONT'D)

8. In the event of a dispute, a designated Auction Official will determine the winning bidder or will re-offer and resell the items in dispute. The Auction Official's decision will be final.

9. An auction official may disqualify the bid on any person blocking the bidding table within 15 minutes prior to closing. The closing bid circled by an auction official will constitute the winning bid. All closing times will be strictly enforced.

LIVE AUCTION RULES

1. All sales are final.

2. The Live Auction will begin after dinner and will continue without interruption until all items have been auctioned.

3. Live Auction items will be displayed throughout the evening.

4. The auctioneer will state any opening bids.

5. To enter a bid, the bidder raises his paddle, directing the signal to the auctioneer or official bid spotters.

6. The highest bidder acknowledged by the

auctioneer shall be the purchaser. In the event of a dispute between bidders, the auctioneer shall have sole and final discretion to determine the successful bidder. No bid, once made, can be withdrawn.

7. The winning bidder will be immediately contacted for presentation of his bid number and concurrence of the amount of the winning bid.

SILENT AUCTION INDEX

Catalogue #	Category
100's	Health, Beauty & Fitness
200's	Services
300's	For the Home
400's	Personal
500's	Sporting Goods
600's	Dinners +
700's	Getaways
800's	Baskets

SILENT AUCTION ITEMS

Health, Beauty and Fitness

Item Number

100 **Facial Refreshment.** Complete facial by "Facial's R' Us." Includes makeup application and free samples of Mary Jo's Cosmetics. *Facial's R' Us.*

101 **Get Fit!** A personal trainer will come to your home, discuss your personal fitness goals, and create an exercise program exclusively for you. This gift includes five (5) one-hour visits. *Built to Last Personal Fitness*

102 **Etc.**

LIVE AUCTION ITEMS

Item Number

1 Dinner with the Head of School. Prepare yourself for the culinary experience of a lifetime. Head of School Albright, assisted by her winsome husband, will prepare in the home of the highest bidder a magnificent meal. Your taste buds will explode when the Albrights serve Italian fare to you and your eight guests.

2 Diamonds and Rubies! A magnificent ruby necklace from Flau's Jewelers. Your loved one will be thrilled when she gazes upon this ruby and diamond necklace with over 3.00 carats of rubies and 2.5 carats of diamonds. Show her how much you love her. This necklace is appraised at $10,350. Opening bid ... $2,500.

3 Etc.

SPONSORS AND DONORS

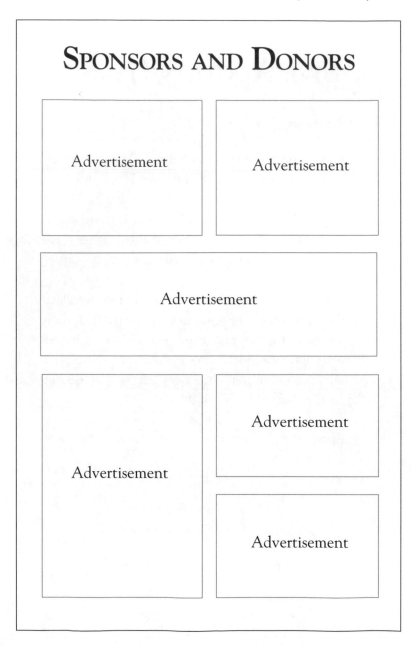

Advertisement

Advertisement

Advertisement

Advertisement

Advertisement

Advertisement

Advertisement

SAMPLE THANK YOU LETTER
TO COMMITTEE MEMBERS

Organization Letterhead

Date:

Dear _____,

I would like to personally thank you for helping to make our fundraising auction a complete success. As you know, we raised $[insert amount].

Your help was instrumental and we hope you'll consider assisting us with next year's auction.

Thank you! Without you we couldn't have done it!

Sincerely,

[Acquisition Committee Chairperson]

DOOR PRIZE REGISTATION SLIPS

DOOR PRIZE REGISTRATION Name:_____ Home Ph._____ Work Ph._____	**DOOR PRIZE REGISTRATION** Name:_____ Home Ph._____ Work Ph._____
DOOR PRIZE REGISTRATION Name:_____ Home Ph._____ Work Ph._____	**DOOR PRIZE REGISTRATION** Name:_____ Home Ph._____ Work Ph._____
DOOR PRIZE REGISTRATION Name:_____ Home Ph._____ Work Ph._____	**DOOR PRIZE REGISTRATION** Name:_____ Home Ph._____ Work Ph._____
DOOR PRIZE REGISTRATION Name:_____ Home Ph._____ Work Ph._____	**DOOR PRIZE REGISTRATION** Name:_____ Home Ph._____ Work Ph._____
DOOR PRIZE REGISTRATION Name:_____ Home Ph._____ Work Ph._____	**DOOR PRIZE REGISTRATION** Name:_____ Home Ph._____ Work Ph._____
DOOR PRIZE REGISTRATION Name:_____ Home Ph._____ Work Ph._____	**DOOR PRIZE REGISTRATION** Name:_____ Home Ph._____ Work Ph._____

TAXES

Fundraising events create tax consequences for guests and for the organization hosting the event. I'll touch on some here, but check with a professional to make sure you're abiding by the laws (federal, state or local) in effect at the time of your auction.

Tax Exemptions for Donors and Buyers

According to the IRS, there are two general rules to be aware of for federal income tax reporting purposes. The first applies to those who provide the gifts, and the second applies to those who purchase the gifts.

1) "A donor is responsible for obtaining a written acknowledgment from a charity for any single contribution of $250 or more before the donor can claim a charitable contribution on his/her federal income tax return."

2) "A charitable organization is required to provide a written disclosure to a donor who receives goods or services in exchange for a single payment in excess of $75."

Let's look at each rule a little more closely.

Written Acknowledgement Requirement

According to the IRS, "A donor cannot claim a tax deduction for any single contribution of $250 or more unless the donor obtains a contemporaneous, written acknowledgment of the contribution from the recipient organization."

An organization that doesn't acknowledge a contribution incurs no penalty; but without a written acknowledgment the donor cannot claim the deduction. Therefore, if you want to maintain good relations, it's a good policy to provide donors with a timely, written statement containing the following information:

1) Name of organization.

2) Amount of cash contribution.

3) Description (but not the value) of non-cash contribution.

4) Statement that no goods or services were provided by the organization in return for the contribution (if that was the case).

5) Description and good-faith estimate of the value of goods or services, if any, that an organization provided in return for the contribution.

6) Statement that goods or services an organization provided, if any, in return for the contribution consisted entirely of intangible benefits (if this was the case).

You can provide a separate acknowledgment for each single contribution of $250 or more, or one acknowledgment, such as an annual summary, that substantiates several single contributions of $250 or more.

As for what the acknowledgment should look like, here's what the IRS has to say:

"There are no IRS forms for the acknowledgment. Letters, postcards, or computer-generated forms with the above information are acceptable. An organization can provide either a paper copy of the acknowledgment to the donor, or an organization can provide the acknowledgment electronically, such as via an e-mail addressed to the donor."

Quid Pro Quo Donations

Occasionally a donor may receive something of value (advertising, a memento) in return for a donation. This is a "quid pro quo" donation.

If you intend to accept quid pro quo donations, you need to be aware of the following requirements:

Goods and Services

Your acknowledgment to the donor must describe the goods or services your organization provided in exchange for a contribution of $250 or more. You must also provide a good faith estimate of the value of such goods or services because a donor must generally reduce the amount of the deduction by the fair market value of the goods and services.

Insubstantial goods or services need not be described in the acknowledgment (a coffee mug, for example). This is known as the token exception rule. Specific dollar amounts apply, for which you'll need to contact the *IRS Exempt Organizations Customer Account Services.*

Examples of Written Acknowledgments

• "Thank you for your cash contribution of $300 that (organization's name) received on December 12, 2010. No goods or services were provided in exchange for your contribution."

• "Thank you for your cash contribution of $350 that (organization's name) received on May 6, 2010. In exchange for your contribution, you received a cookbook with an estimated fair market value of $60."

• "Thank you for your contribution of a used baby crib and matching dresser that (organization's name) charity received on March 15, 2010. No goods or services were provided in exchange for your contribution."

Written Disclosure Requirement

Although many of your guests may believe that what they paid for an item is a pure donation for tax purposes, the donation isn't fully deductible if the item had value (most likely it did). It is considered a "quid pro quo contribution" and you're required, if the payment exceeds $75, to provide donors with written disclosure (a receipt).

Written Disclosures, much like Written Acknowledgements, must contain certain elements. They must:

• Inform a donor that the amount of the contribution deductible for federal income tax purposes is limited to the excess of money (and the fair market value of property other than money) contributed by the donor over the value of goods or services provided by the organization, and

• Provide the donor with a good-faith estimate of the fair market value of the goods or services

A written disclosure statement is not required where the goods or services given to a donor meet the "token exception" rule discussed earlier.

•••

Let me reiterate that because tax laws change frequently you'll want to check with a tax professional (a volunteer, one hopes) before proceeding.

INDEX

Acquisition of gifts
    Committee training, 42
    Process, 44
    Soliciting in person, 44
    Working in teams, 42
    Whom to approach, 42
Ali, Muhammad, 77
Auction catalog, 47-49
Auction night
    Checklists, 78
    Crew, 78
    Depositing money, 79
    Reporting, 80
    Safeguarding money, 79
    Setup, 78
Auction program, 51-55
Auction software, 81-82
Auctions, online, 82-83
Auctioneer, choice of, 16-17
Bacon, Francis, 9
Berle, Milton, 73
Budgeting, 29-31
Checking in, 55-56
Chopra, Deepak, 41
Committees
    Acquisition, 22
    Advertising, 22-23
    Auction catalog, 23
    Checkout, 25
    Decoration and display, 25-26
    Finance, 27
    Invitations, 23
    Live auction, 24
    Miscellaneous revenue
        sources, 26
    Publicity, 25
    Silent auction, 24
    Steering, 21-22
    Thank you, 26

Dauten, Dale, 81
Date, choice of, 14-15
Fleming, Peggy, 12
Gift certificates, 43
Lincoln, Abraham, 33
Live auction
    Bidding process, 64
    Checkout, 68-72
    Getting bidders in the mood, 61
    Number of items to offer, 63
    Opening and minimum bids, 62
    Paddles, 63
    Recording the bidding, 65
    Room layout, 62
    Spotters, 64
Location, choice of, 13-14
Lombardi, Vince, 85
Photography, 18-19
Publicity, 33-35
Refreshments, 18
Revenue sources, additional
    Admission fees, 73
    Advertising, 76
    Beer, wine, cocktails, 74
    Door prizes, 75-76
    Raffles, 75
Roosevelt, Franklin, 19
Silent auction
    Bid sheets, 59
    Gift categories, 57
    Gift display, 58
    Table closing, 59
    Table setup, 58
Speeches, 19
Theme, use of, 15-16
Timeline, 37-39
Truman, Harry 13
Wilde, Oscar, 47

Copies of this and other books from the
publisher are available at discount when
purchased in quantity for boards of directors
or staff. Call 508-359-0019 or visit
www.emersonandchurch.com

Emerson
& Church
PUBLISHERS